The Nell Poems

by

Karin Hoffecker

BLUE LIGHT PRESS ◆ 1ST WORLD PUBLISHING

SAN FRANCISCO ◆ FAIRFIELD ◆ DELHI

The Nell Poems
Copyright ©2018 by Karin Hoffecker

All rights reserved. Printed in the United States of America. No part of this book may be used or reproduced in any manner whatsoever without written permission except in the case of brief quotations embodied in critical articles and reviews. For information contact:

1st World Library
PO Box 2211
Fairfield, IA 52556
www.1stworldpublishing.com

Blue Light Press
www.bluelightpress.com
bluelightpress@aol.com

Book & Cover Design
Melanie Gendron
melaniegendron999@gmail.com

Cover Photo
Jamie Hoffecker

Author Photo
Steve Bartley

First Edition

ISBN 978-1-4218-3807-6

Acknowledgments

Special thanks to Blue Light Press and to Diane Frank and Melanie Gendron for their sound advice and support.

My gratitude to The Southeast Michigan Poetry Meetup Group. Carla Dodd, David Fitch, Marie Davids, Eric Greene, and Nina Robb.

Many thanks to Edward Haworth Hoeppner for his wise and generous counsel.

For Nell and her father who loved her fearlessly.

Contents

Hands 1
Taking Leave 2
At Last 3
Grandmother Fever 5
The Low Tech Life 6
Nesting 7
Her Name 8
Skin Art 10
My California Girl 12
The Parting 14
Under the Surface 16
Brothers 18
Father's Day 20
The Long Goodbye 22
Thin Places 24
Rosemary for Remembrance 25
The Concert 26
In My Life 28
A Unicorn Halloween 29
Play Date 30

About the Author 33

Hands

I remember his hands the day
he was born, big pink fists,
large for a newborn. The doctor

saying, *These are hands
of an athlete.* How as a toddler
his hand clutched mine, soft

chubby fingers warming my
palm. And later, the way our
hands labored side by side

connecting bright Lego bricks
building space capsules, pirate
ships. He reaches for another's

hand now, fingers locked in easy
embrace. Like grandmother's
hands as she dipped pencil-thin

brushes in thick oils marking
canvas: a carriage, church steeple,
blonde boy and his paper boat.

After painting, her hands soapy
at the kitchen sink scouring tin
foil, habit from the Depression.

Hands I reached for the last days
in the nursing home, blue-veined
and small, asleep in her lap.

Taking Leave

He tells me the jasmine
tree is losing leaves,
waxy green petals spill
like tears. Almost lost
to an early freeze, I move
it indoors now. Fragrance
is sweet solace during
winter's ash-gray days.

In Mozambique, a mother
gives birth in the treetop.
Sitting for days, perched
like the chestnut-breasted
robin, the ruby cardinals
living here, each safely
nesting. She finds refuge
from raging waters below:

*"Rock-a-bye baby in the
treetops, when the wind
blows, the cradle will rock"*

I tell my son the jasmine
will survive, when in fall
he takes leave in search
of new roots in strange soil.
When the September sun's
flaxen light wanes, I'll move
the tree inside. In spring my son
will return; the tree will bloom.

At Last

> *"At last, my love has come along,
> my lonely days are over."* — Etta James

This day we celebrate
the long journey —
a decade and a year
in the making. Your union
grounded in the Midwest,
twin oaks steady, tested
by time and travel. From
the arid sun-baked desert
of Arizona, to the misty
Boston Harbor, your branches
entwined, roots embedded,
nourished by rich dark soil.

And now this evening —
of stunning beauty,
you, daughter-in-law
breathtaking in white silk
chiffon gown, an elegant
flower of hand-stitched
petals in your hair. Olive
green heels with jeweled
bows, your signature style.
You son, suddenly a man
in slate seersucker suit,
white dress shirt, pewter
colored tie. The sprig
of lilac blue buds I pin
to your lapel. Remembering
the boy you were.

The two of you between
pedestals of white begonias,
lobelia, the gentle drape
of lysimachia. With exchange
of bands, your pledge to love
and honor. Then first kiss
as husband and wife. Beyond,
the crystal shores of Walloon
Lake, where wind and waves
sing your wedding song . . . .
"And here we are in heaven,
For you are mine at last."

(Kyle and Jamie — July 23, 2011)

Grandmother Fever

It's not that I want to pick up
every baby I see, hug them close,
drink in their milky scent.
But I have grandmother fever.
You know the condition
that comes when friends pull
out candid photos of chubby
blonde-haired babies in red
striped Santa suits, smiles wide.

And when I sit across from you
at Christmas dinner, I wonder
where the tow-headed, brown-eyed
boy went. You are tall and bearded
now, your broad shoulders warm
when you hug me. Where is the boy
who made discoveries in tiny ant
hills, conquered mountains climbing
a playground slide, built Lego castles,
and sculpted ceramic vessels?

You are a man now and I know
the father you will be. I see it when
you hold a child high, push them
on a swing, toss a football in the air.
My daughter-in-law tells me
there'll be a pregnancy in 2014.
Oh, blessed relief from this fever,
to hold a babe against my chest.

The Low Tech Life

I've been thinking a lot
about technology lately.
I won't apologize for being
low tech. No Facebook
account or Twitter, minimal
access to Instagram. I'll never
be one to Skype. I've just
learned to text, take pictures
with my flip phone. I don't
own an iPad Kindle or a Nook
and have no patience for iPhone
users — those who surf the internet,
check e-mail at dinner tables,
take calls in movie theaters.

I think about you, my unborn
grandchild, and the world
you will live in. A society
overrun with social media,
universal operating systems
with layers of transparency
and tracking. Then I think
about the books I'll read to you:
*Goodnight Moon, Pat the Bunny,
The Very Hungry Caterpillar*.
Playgrounds and parks to explore,
sand castles to build, kites to fly.
A quiet life without technology,
our memories face to face.

Nesting
For Jamie (12/6/2014)

At twenty-eight weeks,
she is nesting now.
These last months
a time for gathering

comforts: tiny knit
sweaters and caps,
fleecy pastel blankets,
teethers and lotions.

The stuffed animal
giraffes she adores.
And books, *Curious
George*, the mischievous

monkey my son loved.
Stories I read to him,
our nightly bonding.
Together, you will

make a beautiful nest
strung with lights,
like stars and a moon
warming the night sky.

And laughter, the giddy
joy of your daughter's
voice. A beautiful nest
with song, always song.

Her Name

I tried guessing your name
for months before your birth —
the secret they were keeping.
On walks I would think:

Anna, Aubrey, Avery —
all those A's possible choices.
My daughter-in-law,
worried that she'd let it slip.

Every conversation
was always about Baby Girl,
so often, I decided
your name was *Baby Girl*.

Then, on that frigid March
morning, my son calls to say
they are at the hospital,
so many miles away in Boston.

Two long weeks overdue,
and I am ready for the birth,
ready to know her name.
After sixteen hours, the text

message wakes me and I see
the photo. She is naked, pink
and plump, lying on the hospital
scale. Below the greeting:

Meet Nell Harper, 8 pounds
11 ounces, born at 2:07 a.m.
on 3/6/15. *Nell Harper* —
Nell: the bright, shiny one.

Harper: the harp player.
I think of another Nelle
Harper, *To Kill a Mockingbird*,
a book I love. A beautiful name —

for this new life, my baby girl, Nell.

Skin Art

I remember when it was rare
to see tattoos on anyone

other than Marines, bikers,
or colorful circus roustabouts.

But, I see skin art everywhere —
a butterfly on a shoulder,

the word *Believe* in elegant
cursive on an inside wrist,

the Chinese symbol for crisis
on someone's neck. A tramp

stamp, or a sleeve of skulls
and angry dragons, now trendy.

The daughter of a rocker inks
Stories in black letters on her

shaved head. Michael Phelps has
Olympic rings tattooed on his hip.

My creative friends have had tats
for years: a gingko leaf, a deep

purple plum, the letters *R.E.M.*
scrolled inside a red heart.

My sister's first tattoos: Winnie
the Pooh, a football, the autism

symbol for her children. Now
I have *Nell, 3-6-15,* inked above

my ankle in simple black script
for the granddaughter I treasure.

My California Girl

For Nell on Her First Birthday (3/6/2016)
We do not remember days, we remember moments.
  — *Cesare Pavese*

At eleven months, she's already walking.
Her first steps not a tentative few before
stumbling, but assured as she marches
to the door, whatever's there, the outside

world so inviting. I watch the video dozens
of times, I have to show it to anyone who
asks. Yes, I am that kind of Grandma,
the one who delights in milestones: the first

bath, first tooth, sleeping through the night.
Crawling, how she perfected the army crawl,
arms crossed, elbows propelling her forward
before her knees would do it. Now walking,

her hands wide for balance, a miniature mummy
stepping out. Yesterday, reminiscing about
this time last year, when her mom awaited her
arrival. Passing the time sewing colorful quilts.

I call and we chat about life in California,
the land of lemons and sun. Their new home,
a rambling ranch where my grandbaby loves
to roam. If you turn your back a second, you say,

she'll giddily unroll the toilet paper. In the kitchen,
a wire basket of potatoes she finds fascinating
and tips over. The spuds scattered at her feet.
A stack of glossy magazines too tempting not

to toss; they go merrily on the floor. Today,
the photo of her looking at the sunset,
innocence framed in a brilliant night sky.

We do not remember days, we remember moments.

The Parting
For Kyle (1981-2016)

My beautiful boy is gone. Too young
to leave this life at thirty-four,
still vibrant, so much yet to teach
your daughter. Our precious Nell,

your child in every way: smart,
curious, a big personality at a year
old. The best parts of you left behind.
When she sees your picture and says:

"Da Da," my heart shatters and I am
broken again. Your daughter here
to navigate the world without her father.
My beautiful boy is gone. But I know

the stories I will tell her — you as a boy
who loved mountain biking, Star Wars,
and Coca-Cola. A teen with a passion
for cars. Mercedes, Porsches —

and BMWs, you valeted at the hotel.
That you were an athlete on the football
and lacrosse fields. How you loved
baseball hats worn backwards: MSU,

Lions, the Old English D. A fondness
for T-shirts with words. *Mr. Delicious*,
your signature moniker. And the sweet
nickname you gave her: *The Beeps*.

I will tell her how you loved her mother
fully, heart and soul, how the two of you
were partners in the kitchen, as in all of life.
Your love of eclectic restaurants, craft beer,

and fine wine you enjoyed together
with such zeal. She will know your spirit
of adventure, traveling to Las Vegas,
Vancouver, Montreal, Puerto Rico,

Grand Cayman. And the trip of a lifetime,
around the world in thirty-seven days.
But most of all, I will tell her how deeply
you loved her the first year of her life.

So evident in the abundance of photos.
Moments in time captured of the two
of you: bath time, bedtime, the beach.
You determined to pass your love of water

on, dipping her toes in oceans and lakes
across states north, south, east and west.
And the pictures I hold dearest, you tossing
her in the air arms stretched out to catch her.

Those gentle hands that cradled her when
she was just days old. You running through
the sand with her held like a football,
giddy smiles on both your faces. Standing

side by side at the shore, twin starfish tipped
toward the horizon. A history in pictures,
the first year of her life and the last of yours.
The endless memories of you, my beautiful boy.

Under the Surface

It's been five weeks and the words
still ring in my ears: *collapsed,
pulmonary embolism, he died.*
What I feared the most in my life

has happened. My only child, the son
I adored, gone at thirty-four. I sit
among a stack of cards, sympathy
and condolences from so many.

Two white orchids and a basket of
plants with faded blooms. Their
fragility so much mine. I ask myself
how do I move through the world

with my grief? When others still
talk of parties, doctor's appointments,
summer plans. Does anyone remember
you've died? Some days, I wonder

What's left to go on for? Then I
remember them, daughter-in-law
and granddaughter, the two you loved
so completely in your brief life.

Memories of your last year, our happy
adventures in Boston: restaurants,
museums, shopping excursions. Meals
prepared by the two of you, rivaling

epicurean fare. My 60th birthday
at our beloved Walloon Lake, your last
Christmas, the four generation photo.
New Year's Day, our last goodbye.

The warmth of your embrace, a hug
never forgotten. Jamie gives me
your *Keep Calm and Head Up North*
T-shirt, pictures of you and Nell

on the beach in California, your Apple
business card. Something small but so
treasured. Reminders of your life cut
short. Remembrances of a son adored.

Brothers
For Syed

He is my adopted son now,
your best friend, and I know
you would approve.
When I look in his eyes, the pain
of your death palpable.
This unbelievable loss,
something shared, and I see
our need for one another.

At lunch, we trade stories.
He is sad when you don't
call on his 35th birthday.
He knows you would have
teased him, called him
an "old man," you a year
younger. He tells me about
your trip together, driving
across country, on the way
to your new job in California.

The two of you often lost
touch, business and family
coming first, but when you
pick him up at the airport,
you are back to being Kyle
and Syed. Brothers who'd never
spent a day apart. He tells me
the two of you balanced each
other, his yin to your yang.

Knowing your fears about
becoming a father, he gave
you a pregnancy contract
to sign. And you kept him
focused, inspired him to build
his business. A career in luxury
car sales you would have loved.

He shows me the last photo
of the two of you, taken in Las Vegas,
silly grins on both your faces.
And the photo of the car
he drove, two months after your
death, in the Gold Rush road
rally with the bright red sticker
RIP-KTH. I tell him I am keeping
your memory alive in so many
ways: pictures, poems, the letters
I write to you each week.

I tell him I will be your eyes,
watching your daughter Nell grow
up, recording what you should have
seen for yourself. How thankful
I am that Syed will be a part
of my life in ways he wouldn't
have before your passing. I know
you are watching over us when
the sun bursts through an ash-gray
sky. And in seeing, we celebrate
you, his brother and my son.

Father's Day

For Kyle (June 19, 2016)

It should have been your second
Father's Day, but your unexpected
death has left an echoing loss.
The waves of sadness I feel for

your daughter, Nell, who knew
you for such a brief time. She's
fifteen months and remembers
little of the year you shared,

your bond more precious now.
So I remember that first year
for her. You reciting the bedtime
story by heart. *One hippo all alone,*

calls two hippos on the phone.
Then kneeling, arms curled over
crib railing, watching her sleep.
The two of you dancing with Snoopy,

her bouncing in your lap, swaying
to the musical dog's tune. You
carrying her car seat, "the bucket"
to restaurants. The new foods

you introduced to her: pickles,
avocados, tomatoes, the seafood
you loved. Your excitement seeing
her walk for the first time. Not

a hesitant stroll, but running, arms
wide. And two weeks before you
died, her first birthday, you helping
her with the cake. How you took

her tiny hand in yours, punching
a hole in the layered confection.
The joy of her frosting-filled smile.
I'm sad that I won't see you, years

down the road, delighting in all she
does. Most of all, I am heartbroken
Nell won't experience how beautifully
and deeply you loved her.

Or know the exceptional father you were —
the father I always knew you would be.

The Long Goodbye
For Kyle (August 20, 2016)

I wait until five months after
your death to say goodbye.
The days and weeks unfolding
in waves of grief. The profound

sadness like no other in my life.
I think about what I will miss
and remember about you. What
I will say at the small gathering

of family, as we spread your
ashes in our beloved Walloon
Lake. I will remember your hugs,
your beard, your remarkable

size sixteen feet. Your fondness
for shorts and T-shirts, baseball
hats worn backwards, the seersucker
suit you wore on your wedding day.

Your love of German Chocolate
Cake and East Coast seafood.
Your willingness to try anything
culinary. Your enthusiasm for life

in all you did: craft beer, poker,
cigars. Your love and devotion
to Jamie and Nell, a fierce loyalty
to your friends. The sensitive side

you didn't show many. How you
loved all dogs: Paka, Brewster,
George and Harry. And yes, your
opinion on things. You, not a fan

of Obama, "My President." Your
honesty in choosing to live a life
that made you happy. How you
loved everything cars. Carefully

handwashing and waxing your
BMW baby. Your curiosity
and love of travel. Your loyalty
to your hometown teams: MSU,

Tigers, and Lions. Your expressions —
serious, quirky, giddy. I still hear
your laugh. Your intelligence and
how you taught many so much.

I will miss the excitement of a new
career. The mark you would have
made at Apple. Most of all, I will
miss your love of Walloon Lake.

The decades of swimming, fishing,
jet skiing, boating. Your wedding
by the shore. Now, in the water you
adored, a place to rest my beautiful boy.

Thin Places

In the Celtic Tradition

I look for you in thin places,
where the veil between
heaven and earth is tenuous.

I find you in a narrow sliver
of water and land
that meet. Where the sky
and horizon thread together.

I find you in sacred spaces,
a cement stone of breath
and blessing in the tribute garden.

Your name on the prayer
wall outside the church.

I look for you in thin places,
when sunlight floods the morning.

To know you are the light.

Rosemary for Remembrance

For Jamie

She gives me a rosemary plant
for Mother's Day.

It thrives all summer on a sunny
corner of my deck,
attracting bees and butterflies,
their colorful busyness.

The pungent pine-like scent,
a suggestion of thyme, intoxicating.

I move it indoors when the first frost
of November arrives. Keeping
it hearty, abiding during winter's
long slate-gray months.

I think of the rosemary spice jars,
a keepsake from her bridal shower.
Rosemary for remembrance, sea salt
for flavor in life, citrus for zest.

Gone now, I remember our beautiful
boy. Like the spices, the savory flavor
of how he lived.

The Concert

It was a birthday gift from my
sisters planned months in advance.
The 80's British band Depeche
Mode, the headliner. I delight

in the music, the lights, how
alive I feel inside. The first time
since my son's death. The electronic
songs ring in my ears as we leave.

We wind our way through the throng
of people departing and I fall behind.
It's then when I see him sitting
in a wheelchair, at a sly distance,

and I want to run from this secret.
But his profile so familiar, my curiosity
sends me forward around the chair,
and I know now it's John. The one

I met at the dance club that played
Depeche Mode, the one I lived
with for twelve years, the one who
was more father to my son than his own.

He says he fractured his ankle
in a fall. I touch his knee, tell him
he's too old to be on ladders. He raises
his arms and I bend to hug him. Our

breakup, long since forgiven. I walk
away knowing I will see him again.
If only to talk about music and art,
talk about our lives then and now.

To reminisce about the boy we loved.

In My Life

Title and Lyrics by John Lennon

It's John Lennon's birthday today,
the radio the playlist of songs
remembering him: *Imagine,
Give Peace a Chance, In My Life.*

I remember the news reports
on the night he died. The lone
gunman shooting him in the back,
in the archway of the Dakota Hotel.

It's December 8, 1980 and the world
mourns. His melodies and lyrics
silenced forever. A year later to the day,
you, son, come bellowing into my life.

Red-faced, fists clenched, your song
the most beautiful in the world.
I took for granted then, the music
of your voice would never cease.

I loved your singing as a child,
the deep baritone of you, the man.
Like Lennon, you were taken too soon.
Just thirty-four when the music died.

Tonight his lyrics cradle my heart:
*Though I know I'll never lose affection
For people and things that went before
I know I'll often stop and think about them
In my life I love you more*

Oh, my son, I love you more.

A Unicorn Halloween
Detroit Zoo, October 20, 2017

At the Zoo Boo, my granddaughter
is dressed as a pink and white unicorn.
A fuchsia mane running down her back,
her spiral horn swirls to the sky.

In the photo she is posed beside a sculpture,
a black otter lounging across a log.

I see her impish smile, her father's eyes.

I remember Halloweens with him,
trips to the pumpkin patch.

Hayrides in a straw-filled wagon
wandering through fields the color of a sunrise,
looking for the perfect jack-o'-lantern.

His costumes always homemade:
Army soldier, Ninja, Freddy Krueger.

He carried an old pillowcase for collecting
his bounty. After trick-or-treating, he sprawled
on the floor, counting his riches.
Fun-sized Skittles and Snickers
clear winners in the Halloween sweepstakes.

Now, he is gone too soon. Only one Halloween
shared with his daughter.
He will miss the spooky moonlit nights,
his little unicorn, her chocolate kisses.

Play Date

She marches in for our weekly play date,
abandons her coat and runs across the room
shouting, "Come Grandma Karin. Read a book."
We begin with *Where's Spot*, look under all

the flaps, find him in the wicker basket. She
turns the page and says, "The End." Then, it's
coloring, me with crayons, her with pencils.
We trace her hand, her round chubby fingers.

Decorate the design with stickers: birds, bees,
dogs, and kittens. We try baby yoga. She spreads
her arms in butterfly wings, curls like a sleeping
mouse, crouches, as a frog who says,

"ribbit, ribbit." Always hungry after day care,
my snack shelf grows: apple juice, crackers,
blueberry puffs. "More please," when the cup
is empty. In quiet moments, we sit side by side

on the couch and cuddle. I call her my sweetie
pie, kiss her silky hair, drink its clean scent.
I show her the doll I have for her. She says, "Baby
Georgia." All her dolls are named Georgia. I smile

as she undresses her, removes her pajamas and pink
hat. "Naked baby," she squeals in delight. We look
at photos around the house. "Who's that?" she asks
pointing to my nieces and nephew at her young age.

She picks up a frame with "Mama" and the daddy
she has half-forgotten, a year since his passing.
I long for the days when she is older, to tell her about
her father who loved her so fearlessly. She studies

the picture intently and kisses it saying, "Mama."
And when I look at her face, I see you, my beautiful
boy, the same eyes, your smile and giddy laughter.
This precious piece of you that I love so deeply.

She will be a two-year-old soon, and I have
cherished her this last year. Watched with delight,
a curious mind seeing the world around her. So focused
for someone still so young. A vocabulary exploding

along with her independence: "Nell do it." When
our play date is over, I bundle her up and buckle the car
seat with her help. "I did it. Go see Mama." Singing us
home to Mama with the *ABC's, Twinkle, Twinkle*

Little Star. Every word sung from memory. When we
say goodbye, she looks at me and says, "sweetie pie."
Yes, oh yes, Nell, you are my sweetie pie. I hear our
voices echoing under a brilliant, blue March sky.

About the Author

Karin Hoffecker has an MA in English Literature from Oakland University, Rochester, Michigan. Her poems have appeared in *Penumbra, The Comstock Review, The MacGuffin, Mona Poetica, Passager,* and *Peninsula Poets.* Fascinated with the visual arts and the natural world as subjects, she explores them often in her poetry. She is a retired teacher who is devoted to the practice of yoga and spending time with her granddaughter Nell, for whom these poems were written. She lives in Birmingham, Michigan.